GO FOR IT!

Workbook

BY: DONNA DICK CONNOR

ISBN: 978-1-962656-45-0

CONTENTS

INTRODUCTION

Hello, my fellow Go-Getters!

Welcome to the **GO FOR IT!** Workbook.

This is your companion (sold separately) to the best-selling book Go For It! How Anyone Can Achieve Their Dreams. This workbook has been created to allow you the space to go deep into everything you want in life and work through how to get it.

This is your place to dig in, write about your thoughts, goals, and dreams, to look at what might hold you back and how to get around the potholes that might appear on your journey. You can DECIDE what you want to Do, Have, and Become in this life. Think BIG! Don't let any negative thoughts stop you from dreaming. Don't worry about what anyone else might think during this process. The only thing limiting you here is your own dreams and desires. You won't think of everything in one sitting. Use this book to continually add to your list of what you want to achieve in life. You'll get more ideas as you do the work and hear what others are doing. Add to your list over and over. Enjoy this experience.

All you need to create YOUR dream life is to learn the steps to achieve whatever you want, then rinse and repeat.

This workbook has been designed as a place to break through and move forward. To create YOUR Dream Life that you design.

My intention with this workbook is to give you a dedicated place to do the work, activate your creativity, get in touch with your true desires, and create a massive vision of what your life could be like if you...**Go For It!**

I can't wait to see what you DECIDE to achieve!

How to use the Go For It! Workbook:

1. Read a chapter in the Go For It! Book
2. Open this companion workbook and do the work for the coordinating chapter
3. Answer the questions and do the assignments

I have taken the questions throughout each chapter of the book and placed them here for you with space to do the homework right here. I have left you additional space at the end of each chapter to write additional notes, record your research on whatever you want to achieve, journal about your journey, or add your musings to anything on your mind.

The Go For It! Book and this Companion Workbook will teach you to see your life with more possibilities. To believe in yourself and trust that you already have everything you need inside of yourself to accomplish everything you want. It will open your minds to see and create more opportunities than you ever imagined. You will learn to use your mind to create all you want to achieve.

This book will change the trajectory of your life if you do the work!

That's why I wrote, Go For It!...
This matters. Your life matters. Your future matters. How you empower those around you matters.

"...pursuing your dreams can also inspire and motivate others. By following your passions and achieving your goals, you can be a role model and show others that anything is possible if you are willing to work for it and believe in yourself. Your success can inspire others to pursue their own dreams and create a ripple effect of positive change in the world."

Don't hide what you are doing, the goals you are achieving, or the dreams you are pursuing. Be a light of encouragement for others to go after their dreams!

With love and excitement, I send you on your journey to self-discovery!

ENJOY the adventure!

Donna
XO

INTRODUCTION

Read the Introduction. Then, answer the following questions.

The key takeaway here is the importance of mastering the art of mental decluttering. When we avoid unsettling thoughts and suppress underlying fears, they often amplify to grab our attention. By developing the skill to confront and process these inner concerns, we create room within ourselves. This newfound mental space can then be harnessed deliberately to steer our thoughts, emotions, and energy towards manifesting our dreams.

WHAT FEARS DO YOU HAVE ABOUT GETTING WHAT YOU WANT IN LIFE?

WHAT IS YOUR SUPERPOWER?

We all have them…mine, is I have NEVER lost a sock in the dryer. Never. Lol. It's true, but I'm talking about real superpowers here. I can streamline processes to avoid redundancies and prevent extra work.

WHAT DON'T YOU KNOW RIGHT NOW THAT YOU WISH YOU DID?

IS THERE SOMETHING YOU HAVE "FAILED AT" ALREADY BUT CAN SEE HOW MUCH YOU LEARNED FROM THE EXPERIENCE?

WHAT INTERESTS DO YOU HAVE RIGHT NOW?

WHAT ARE YOUR CURRENT DREAMS AND DESIRES?

WHAT CRAZY AND WILD DREAMS DO YOU HAVE BUT JUST CAN'T SEE EVER COMING TO FRUITION?

NOTES:

NOTES:

NOTES:

NOTES:

CHAPTER ONE:

YOUR DREAM LIFE PLAN

Read Chapter Two. Then start designing YOUR Dream Life Plan.

WHAT IS IMPORTANT TO YOU?

WHAT ARE YOUR VALUES THAT HELP YOU NAVIGATE LIFE?

WHAT ARE YOU MOST PASSIONATE ABOUT?

Now it's time to make your **Dream List**. Fill these areas out of what you want to Do, Have, and Become. This is YOUR list. Don't worry if you think someone will be mad at you for wanting it. Write it down. Nothing bad will happen for wanting it. Write it down. Don't worry about whether or not you think you can actually achieve it. Write it down.

YOUR DREAM LIST...

1 WHAT DO YOU WANT TO DO?

CONTINUED ON NEXT PAGE...

2 WHAT DO YOU WANT TO HAVE?

3 WHAT DO YOU WANT TO BECOME?

WHAT CAME UP FOR YOU AS YOU MADE YOUR DREAM LIST?

List the good, the bad, the ugly.

NOTICE WHAT YOUR LIMITING BELIEFS SAY YOU CAN'T HAVE.

List them all out and then invalidate each and every one with ideas that feel better and support your dreams and desires.

WHOSE VOICE CAME UP SAYING YOU CAN'T DO THESE THINGS?

We all have them. It's okay. The important thing here is to recognize that most naysayers (in their minds) only do it to protect you. They can't imagine doing what you want to do and want to keep you from getting hurt. Appreciate that they care for you enough to worry. Then...Let it go!

WHO ARE THE PEOPLE YOU FEAR WILL JUDGE YOU FOR TAKING THIS JOURNEY?

Make your list. Who do you think will judge you, and why do you think they will?

WHAT IF THEY DO JUDGE YOU?

What is the worst that can happen? Can you live with that? Does it matter if they do? Do you want what you want bad enough to quit worrying about being judged?

DECIDE WHAT YOU WANT YOUR LIFE TO LOOK LIKE.

Take some time to write a story about your life. What do have have? What does your perfect day look like? What do you do? Who do you spend your time with? Go deep into the details. Really see it. Walk through your dream home and describe it. Describe your dream family and what you want. Describe your dream career or business or hobby. You get the idea. The mind is VISUAL. Write it out. Then come back and read this daily! Let your mind envision what you want, and it will help you create it.

CONTINUED ON NEXT PAGE...

WHAT WOULD YOU BE THINKING, AND WHAT WOULD YOU BE FEELING IF YOU ALREADY HAD EVERYTHING YOU WANTED?

Write it down and feel it as if you already had it all.

NOTES:

NOTES:

NOTES:

NOTES:

CHAPTER TWO:

DECIDING WHAT YOU WANT TO DO, HAVE, AND BECOME

After you've read chapter two, it is time to DECIDE! Let's narrow your list and choose the first goal to start your journey to creating YOUR Dream Life Plan.

Look at your lists. Read each and every item you wrote down. Imagine having each one. What does your life look like? How does it feel?

WRITE DOWN YOUR TOP FIVE MOST IMPORTANT THINGS IN EACH CATEGORY:

WHAT DO I WANT TO DO?

WHAT DO I WANT TO HAVE?

WHAT DO I WANT TO BECOME?

yay!

PHEW! HOW WAS THAT EXPERIENCE?

Did you go back and forth? Did you already know which five seemed right? How did you make your decisions?

Now it's time to narrow down the lists again.

WRITE DOWN HERE YOUR TOP TWO MOST IMPORTANT ONES IN EACH CATEGORY

WHAT DO I WANT TO DO?

WHAT DO I WANT TO HAVE?

WHAT DO I WANT TO BECOME?

PHEW, AGAIN! HOW WAS THAT EXPERIENCE?

Was it easier or harder this time? Did you go back to your list and reevaluate things?

Now it's time to narrow down the lists **again**.

WRITE DOWN HERE YOUR TOP MOST IMPORTANT ONE IN EACH CATEGORY

WHAT DO I WANT TO DO?

WHAT DO I WANT TO HAVE?

WHAT DO I WANT TO BECOME?

IT. IS. TIME!

Out of the three items you listed as the most important for you, which one do you want to go after right now and start your journey?

CHOOSE YOUR FIRST JOURNEY:

Pick the ONE goal you want to focus on right NOW.

WHY DID YOU CHOOSE THIS ONE THING?

CHOOSE ROUTE:

WHAT ARE THE MACRO STEPS TO ACCOMPLISH THIS GOAL?

It's okay if you don't know all the steps, or even the first one. It's time to research and start writing down what you must do to accomplish it.

WHAT ARE THE MICRO STEPS TO ACCOMPLISH THIS GOAL?

CHOOSE YOUR SPEED LIMIT:

HOW FAST CAN THIS GOAL ACTUALLY BE ACCOMPLISHED?

Yes, we all want what we want right now, but we also know it will take at least seven years to become a lawyer or 10,000 hours to master a new skill, so let's be realistic with ourselves and set some reasonable timeframes. If you are a single mom working two jobs, it will take you longer to get through school than a newly graduated high school student who doesn't have to work. And that is okay! We're all at different stages. You do you. You worry about your journey and don't compare or fret that your journey will look different than someone else's.

CHOOSE YOUR REFUELING STOPS:

WHAT DO YOU NEED TO LEARN TO ACCOMPLISH THIS GOAL?

DO YOU NEED TO ATTEND SCHOOL, TAKE A COURSE, HIRE A COACH, OR READ A BOOK?

CHOOSE YOUR TRAVEL COMPANIONS:

WHO ARE YOU BRINGING ALONG ON THIS JOURNEY?

WHY DO YOU WANT THEM TO JOIN YOU?

CAN THEY HELP YOU ON YOUR JOURNEY?

CHOOSE YOUR SIDE TRIPS:

Make a list of ways to reward yourself after you hit certain mile markers on your journey.

INVITE OTHERS TO GO ON THIS JOURNEY WITH YOU:

Make a list of who you want and who you need to take on this journey.

WHY DO YOU WANT THEM TO COME?

WHAT HELP WILL THEY PROVIDE?

WHAT'S IN IT FOR THEM?

EXCESS BAGGAGE:

WHAT IS WEIGHING YOU DOWN AND STOPPING YOU FROM REACHING YOUR DESTINATION?

Are you in debt? Do you need to work through any fears and anxiety? Do you need to get out of your own way? Do you need to ask someone NOT to join you on your journey?
Write it all down.

ARRIVAL:

WHAT CAN YOU DO ONCE YOU ARRIVE AT YOUR GOAL?

WHAT ARE THE FEELINGS YOU WANT TO FEEL?

WHAT IS THE PURPOSE OF THE JOURNEY?

HELPING OTHERS ON THEIR JOURNEYS:

HOW CAN YOU PAY IT FORWARD?

HOW CAN YOU MENTOR OTHERS ON THEIR JOURNEYS?

HOW DO YOU WANT TO GIVE BACK?

YOUR WHY:

WHY DO YOU WANT TO ACCOMPLISH THIS GOAL?

WHAT ISSUES MAY COME UP FOR YOU ON THIS JOURNEY?

Perhaps you don't have enough money to accomplish the goal, or you lack support. You might not do as well in school, or your business won't take off as quickly as you hoped.

WHAT ARE THE SOLUTIONS FOR THOSE ISSUES?

How can you earn more money? How can you surround yourself with more support? How can you get help if you start struggling in school? What are ways to help your business grow?

BRAVO!

You've now laid everything out for this journey. You know where you're going and how you are going to get there. You know who is coming with you and where you will stop to refuel. **Now it's time to put the car in gear and move forward.**

WHAT IS THE FIRST STEP YOU NEED TO TAKE ON THIS JOURNEY?

What is the deadline for this step? What is the SECOND step? What is the deadline for this step? ***Fill out the table below with the first steps that need to happen.***

STEPS	DEADLINE
1	
2	
3	
4	
5	
6	
7	
8	
9	
10	

NOTES:

NOTES:

NOTES:

NOTES:

CHAPTER THREE:

INCLUDING OTHERS IN YOUR JOURNEY

In the last chapter, you chose who you want to take on this journey. Now it's time to talk to them about it. Use this chapter to answer the questions in it and write out your first dream more clearly. Write out what you'd like to share with those you want to invite, why you want them to accompany you, and how you see them in your dream life. The more you prepare your thoughts here, the easier the conversation will go because you have fully thought things through.

1. TELL THEM YOUR DREAM

Write it out in detail. Not just the one sentence in the last chapter. Write it out in full. What does it look like? Describe your life once you've achieved this dream. Get really clear on it.

2. HANDLE OBJECTIONS

You can write out all the objections they might have and prepare a response here. This isn't to be argumentative, but a great way to think about things from every angle and to find your own answers. The more prepared you are to answer their questions, the more comfortable they will be. And be prepared for them not to understand right away or to have concerns. It's alright. They care about you. Have them share their thoughts without becoming defensive. Thank them for caring enough about you to share their thoughts. Ask them what they would see for you. (You don't have to take the advice, but listen because you will likely garner great information.)

CONTINUED ON NEXT PAGE...

3. TELL THEM WHAT'S IN IT FOR THEM

List all your ideas out here.

4. INVITE THEM TO SIT IN A SPECIFIC SEAT IN YOUR JOURNEY AND ASK THEM WHERE THEY WANT TO SIT

It may match or it may not. That's okay. Work through it.

5. ALLOW THEM TO WORK ON YOUR DREAM WITH YOU

They will most likely have insights and ideas you haven't thought about yet

6. RECIPROCATE!

Ask them about their dreams and how you can support them

7. WORK ON YOUR DREAMS TOGETHER AND CELEBRATE TOGETHER!

NOTES:

NOTES:

NOTES:

NOTES:

CHAPTER FOUR:

THE SECRETS TO REACHING YOUR GOALS FASTER

Read chapter four. Start thinking about why you want to reach this goal and answer the questions in the chapter to really understand how you can reach your goal and activate your brain working with you to accomplish it.

WHAT DO I WANT? (CURRENT GOAL - WRITE IT OUT IN DETAIL AGAIN)

WHY DO I AND MY FAMILY WANT THIS?

WHO BENEFITS FROM ME GETTING THIS?

KEEP IT UP!

WHEN CAN I GET THIS DONE?

WHERE CAN I DO THIS?

WHAT AM I WILLING TO SACRIFICE TO ACCOMPLISH THIS?

ALMOST THERE!

HOW CAN I DO THIS?

LET'S DIG DEEPER ON YOUR WHY...

I'm going to ask you why you want to accomplish your goal. Then I'm going to ask you why several more times to really dig deep, like I demonstrated in the book.

WHY?

WHY DO YOU WANT TO ACCOMPLISH THIS GOAL?

WHY?

WHY?

WHY?

WHY?

WHY?

WHY?

WHY?

DECLARATIONS

CREATE A LIST OF ONE-WORD DECLARATIONS THAT HAVE MEANING FOR YOU

CREATE A LIST OF ONE-SENTENCE DECLARATIONS THAT HAVE MEANING FOR YOU

CREATE A LIST OF MULTIPLE SENTENCE DECLARATIONS THAT HAVE MEANING FOR YOU

VISION BOARD ITEMS

WHAT DO YOU WANT ON YOUR VISION BOARD RIGHT NOW?

MORNING ROUTINE

WHAT DO I DO FOR MY MORNING ROUTINE?

WHAT ARE THE RULES I WILL LIVE BY?

COACHES

WHAT SKILLS COULD I USE TO BENEFIT ME ON MY JOURNEY THAT I MIGHT WANT TO HIRE A COACH FOR?

(ie. Mindset, productivity, money, etc.)

WHO COACHES ON THAT SKILL SET?

DO I NEED THEM NOW OR LATER?

WHAT WILL IT COST?

DO I HAVE THAT MONEY NOW, OR WILL I SAVE UP FOR IT?

NOTES:

NOTES:

NOTES:

NOTES:

CHAPTER FIVE:

THE LAW OF THE MIRROR

After reading chapter five, look in the mirror and reflect on your life. Be honest with yourself and see if there is room for improvement. Are there things you are doing that are not helping you reach your new goal? If there is, start working on making those changes now and see how quickly things improve for you.

HOW ARE YOU BEING TREATED IN LIFE?

WHAT ARE YOU PROJECTING?

WHAT CHANGES DO YOU NEED TO MAKE TO SEE MORE SUCCESS IN YOUR LIFE?

HOW IS YOUR SELF-ESTEEM?

HOW DO YOU SEE YOURSELF?

WHAT VALUE DO YOU SEE IN YOURSELF?

WHAT MIGHT BE LACKING THAT YOU COULD BE WORKING ON RIGHT NOW?

WHAT CAUSED IT?

HOW CAN YOU LOOK AT IT DIFFERENTLY?

NOTES:

NOTES:

NOTES:

NOTES:

CHAPTER SIX:

HOW YOUR ATTITUDE & FEELINGS DETERMINE YOUR FINANCIAL SUCCESS

Read chapter six and then understand what your feelings about money are, how you got them, and if it's time to let go of ideas that don't work for you anymore.

WHAT WERE YOU TAUGHT ABOUT MONEY GROWING UP?

Both verbally and by what was demonstrated to you

HOW WAS MONEY DISCUSSED IN YOUR HOME?

WHAT THOUGHTS AND FEELINGS DID YOUR FAMILY HAVE ABOUT MONEY?

Good/evil, valuable/worthless, hard to get/easy to come by, real/imaginary.

HOW ARE THOSE THOUGHTS AND FEELINGS ABOUT MONEY WORKING FOR YOU RIGHT NOW?

HOW WOULD YOU LIKE TO FEEL ABOUT MONEY?

WHAT IS STOPPING YOU FROM CHANGING HOW YOU FEEL ABOUT MONEY?

WRITE OUT IN-DEPTH HOW YOU WANT TO FEEL ABOUT AND ACT TOWARD MONEY.

NOTES:

NOTES:

NOTES:

NOTES:

CHAPTER SEVEN:

FINANCIAL LITERACY BASICS

Read chapter seven. Take time to learn the terms so you feel comfortable that you understand them. Think of people who are great examples of how to handle money.

WHAT DO YOU WISH YOU KNEW MORE ABOUT MONEY AND FINANCES?

WHERE CAN YOU FIND THOSE ANSWERS?

WHO DO YOU WANT TO EMULATE WHEN IT COMES TO MONEY?

WHAT ARE THEY DOING THAT YOU WISH YOU WERE DOING?

WHAT ARE THEY NOT DOING THAT YOU WISH YOU WOULD STOP DOING?

WHAT CAN YOU DO RIGHT NOW TO IMPROVE YOUR UNDERSTANDING OF HOW MONEY WORKS?

NOTES:

NOTES:

NOTES:

NOTES:

CHAPTER EIGHT:

INTEREST NEVER SLEEPS

Ahhh, interest. After reading chapter eight, take a good look at your own finances. Answer the questions and see what improvements can and should be made to improve your situation and create a solid financial foundation to go after your dream.

WHAT ARE YOU PAYING INTEREST ON RIGHT NOW?

HOW CAN YOU PAY THOSE THINGS OFF QUICKLY?

(See Chapter 9 exercises.)

WHAT INVESTMENTS ARE YOU MISSING OUT ON NOW BECAUSE YOU'RE PAYING INTEREST ON OTHER THINGS?

HOW CAN YOU CHANGE THAT?

NOTES:

NOTES:

NOTES:

NOTES:

CHAPTER NINE:

HOW TO INVEST IN YOUR FUTURE

Read chapter nine and start thinking of the numerous ways to invest in your future. The best way to invest is to find something that interests you. If you don't love it, you won't care for it how it needs to be cared for and managed. There is no right or wrong answer here. And it's okay to change your mind as you learn more strategies and get more education, or try things and realize that you don't enjoy it as much as you thought you might.

WHEN YOU THINK OF INVESTING, WHAT INTERESTS YOU MOST?

WHAT ARE YOUR THOUGHTS ON INVESTING IN THE STOCK MARKET?

WHAT DO YOU THINK ABOUT USING REAL ESTATE AS AN INVESTMENT TOOL?

DO YOU WANT TO OWN YOUR OWN BUSINESS?

WHAT KIND OF BUSINESS INTERESTS YOU?

WHAT DO YOU NEED TO LEARN TO INVEST THE WAY YOU WOULD LIKE?

WHO CAN HELP YOU?

NOTES:

NOTES:

NOTES:

NOTES:

CHAPTER TEN:

YOUR DREAM FINANCIAL TOOLS

Read chapter ten then download and start using Your Dream Financial Tools
http://www.go.lifeonpurposeacademy.com/gfitools

Watch the training videos and create the financial foundation you want and need to achieve every dream you listed earlier in this workbook.

DO YOU FEEL ANY HESITANCY ABOUT GETTING YOUR FINANCES IN ORDER?

If so, what is it?

WHERE IS IT COMING FROM?

HOW CAN YOU OVERCOME THESE ISSUES?

WHY YOU DON'T WANT TO DO THIS

THE BENEFITS OF DOING IT SO YOU CAN REACH YOUR GOALS

NOTES:

NOTES:

NOTES:

NOTES:

CHAPTER ELEVEN:

LIFE IS A HIGHWAY

After reading chapter eleven, list ways to celebrate your wins throughout your journey.

When you have something to look forward to, it keeps you motivated. And, only some ways to celebrate need to cost money. Take some downtime to read for pleasure instead of work, or take a day to be in nature and unwind.

LIST ALL THE THINGS YOU WOULD LIKE TO DO TO REWARD YOURSELF FOR HITTING KEY MILESTONES ON YOUR JOURNEY:

WHAT ARE SOME POTHOLES THAT YOU CAN ALREADY IDENTIFY MIGHT COME UP AS YOU GO AFTER THIS GOAL?

WHAT ARE SOME POSSIBLE SOLUTIONS FOR EACH OF THESE POTHOLES?

Planning ahead sometimes eliminates them altogether. In the least, it helps you prepare, not be so caught off guard and gets your mind thinking faster.

WHAT EMOTIONS ARE COMING UP ABOUT GOING AFTER THIS FIRST GOAL?

You may be feeling overwhelmed, angry, sad, or even numb. All of these emotions are valid and normal in response to a curve ball. Take time to process your feelings, but also try not to get lost in them. It's important to strike a balance between acknowledging your emotions and not letting them consume you.

MAKE A LIST OF RESOURCES YOU NEED FOR THIS JOURNEY.
IE. FRIENDS, FAMILY, COACHES, FINANCING, ETC.

RESOURCE	WHAT IS NEEDED	WHY IT'S NEEDED

NOTES:

NOTES:

NOTES:

NOTES:

CHAPTER TWELVE:

LIVING YOUR LIFE ON PURPOSE

Understanding what is important to you helps you stay aligned with every decision you make. Take some time here to understand what your values are and how they play a key role in creating YOUR Dream Life.

WHAT DO YOU VALUE IN LIFE?

WHAT BRINGS YOU JOY AND FULFILLMENT IN LIFE?

WHAT ARE YOUR STRENGTHS, AND HOW CAN YOU USE THEM TO CONTRIBUTE TO THE WORLD?

HOW CAN YOU ALIGN YOUR ACTIONS WITH YOUR VALUES?

HOW CAN YOU FIND FULFILLMENT ON THIS JOURNEY, EVEN DURING A ROUGH TIME?

NOTES:

NOTES:

NOTES:

NOTES:

CHAPTER THIRTEEN:

WHAT'S NEXT

I encourage you to take the information and understanding you have gained in the Go For It! book along with the insights, dreams, and decisions you created in this workbook and really...

GO FOR IT!!!

YOU ARE MEANT TO HAVE YOUR DREAM LIFE!

YOUR LIFE ON PURPOSE AWAITS YOU!

YOU ARE WORTHY, POWERFUL, AND CAPABLE OF ACHIEVING EVERY DREAM YOU LISTED IN THIS WORKBOOK!

THIS IS JUST THE BEGINNING FOR YOU!!

I AM HERE WITH ALL THE ENCOURAGEMENT, MOTIVATION, AND RESOURCES YOU NEED!

DONNA
XO

Schedule a clarity call to see how we can help you on this journey you are about to embark on.
https://calendly.com/lifeonpurposeacademyut/clarity

Join our free Facebook Group - Going For It!
https://www.facebook.com/groups/goingforit/

Check out our coaching program that can support you on your journey to achieve every dream you have.
https://go.lifeonpurposeacademy.com/goforitcoaching

YOUR ROADMAP FOR YOUR DREAM LIFE PLAN

Here is a quick summary of your roadmap for everything you want to create YOUR Dream Life Plan.

1. Create your dream list of everything you want to do, have, or become.
2. DECIDE! You've made your list... Now, decide your number one goal and create your roadmap.
3. Create the list of steps it's going to take to reach your goal. Break those steps down further into manageable tasks.
4. Make a list of everyone you need to get on board with your goal and have those discussions
5. Work on your mindset throughout your journey.
6. Create a solid financial foundation to reach your goal.
7. Enjoy the journey!
8. Celebrate the small wins along the way!
9. Be proud of yourself for reaching your goal!
10. Rinse and repeat with your next goal and your next one until you have created your ultimate dream life.

RESOURCES

People I Love to Work With

Richie Norton

Read the books, The Power of Starting Something Stupid, and Anti-Time Management

Sign up for this 76-Day Challenge to make your STUPID idea Your SMART Reality at http://richienorton.com/76daychallenge/

Kirk and Kim Duncan

Check out his Master Your Influence group coaching at https://3keyelements.com/master-your-influence-join-today/

Listen to any of his audiobook trainings at https://3keyelements.com/audiobook-library/

Natasha Hazlett

Check her out at https://natashahazlett.com

Join her next 5-day Unstoppable Influence Challenge at https://unstoppableInfluence.idevaffiliate.com/2194.html

Michael Yeung

Check out his website at https://www.eliteproductivity.io/

Join his free Facebook group at www.facebook.com/groups/teamppe

COMPLETE LIST OF BOOKS I RECOMMEND BY CHAPTER

This section features affiliate links, meaning I will earn a small commission if you purchase through these links.

The Go-Giver **by Bob Burg**

The Richest Man in Babylon by George S. Clason

The Power of Starting Something Stupid by Richie Norton

How to Win Friends and Influence People by Dale Carnegie

Crucial Conversations: Tools for Talking When Stakes are High
by Kerry Patterson

Unstoppable Influence: Be You. Be Fearless. Transform Lives.
by Natasha Hazlett

The Perfect Day Formula by Craig Ballantyne

The 15 Invaluable Laws of Growth: Live Them and Reach Your Potential
by John C. Maxwell

Attitude 101 by John C Maxwell

The Truth About Money by Ric Edelman

Rich Dad Poor Dad by Robert Kiyosaki

The Power of Zero by David McKnight

Financial Peace by Dave Ramsey

You've Got This! by Will Matthews

ADDITIONAL BOOKS I LOVE THAT WILL HELP YOU ON YOUR JOURNEY

Anti-Time Management by Richie Norton

Psycho-Cybernetics by Maxwell Maltz

OTHER LINKS INCLUDED THROUGHOUT THE BOOK

Chapter 3:
Video: Authenticity vs Attachment by Dr. Gabor Maté

Chapter 4:
Vision Board Training

Chapter 8:
The Power of Zero Documentary

Chapter 9:
Charles Schwab Investor Profile Questionnaire

Schedule a free, no-obligation appointment to review your personal finances and discuss your investment strategies to reach your goals here:

Chapter 10:
Dream Life Plan financial tools.
Each tool has a video training on how to use it.

DONNA CONNOR

Made in the USA
Monee, IL
02 November 2026

67376097R00079